On Home Meetings

Witness Lee

Living Stream Ministry
Anaheim, California

©Witness Lee

First Edition, 6,250 copies. October 1986.

Library of Congress Catalog
Card Number: 86-82418

ISBN 0-87083-256-5 (hardcover)
ISBN 0-87083-257-3 (softcover)

Published by

Living Stream Ministry
1853 W. Ball Road, P. O. Box 2121
Anaheim, CA 92804 U.S.A.

Printed in the United States of America

CONTENTS

PREFACE

The messages contained in this book concerning the home meetings were given as a series of training messages in April, 1985 in Taipei, Taiwan. They have been translated from the Chinese.

CHAPTER ONE

THE FOUNDATION OF THE CHURCH MEETINGS

Scripture Reading: Acts 2:42, 46, 47; 5:42; 1 Cor. 14:23a, 26

FIVE ITEMS PLUS ONE ITEM OF SPIRITUAL WORK

Last time, we had a completely new arrangement of the church in Taipei. On the one hand, on the administrative side, we arranged to have over forty elders to take the lead in the halls. On the other hand, regarding the spiritual work, there were five items plus one. The burden of the five items is to be shared by the full-time co-workers. There is one more item, the burden of which is to be shared by the brothers and sisters in each hall. The co-workers should take the lead to carry out the five items of spiritual work. The first is the campus gospel work, the second is the home meetings, the third is the home gospel, the fourth is the gospel to all levels of society, and the fifth is the children's work. There is one more item, which is visitation and shepherding. This item is reserved for each meeting hall and should be done by all the brothers and sisters under the elders' leadership. These are the six items of spiritual work. Simply speaking, if the church is to be built up and move forward, to grow spiritually, to know the truth, and to bear fruit in the gospel, there must be the elders' leadership on the administrative side, and the six items of spiritual work on the spiritual side: the campus gospel work, the home meetings, the home gospel, the gospel to all levels of society, the children's work, plus the visitation and shepherding in each hall.

A Living Person Climbing a Steep Slope

Last time, I could only make a start because I had to return quickly to the United States. I really had the burden to go on further, so tonight we will pick up where we left off last time and move forward once again. Let us first talk about the matter of home meetings. Although having home meetings sounds easy, from the first day we began I knew that it would be harder to do well in this matter than in all other matters. It is surely difficult to climb up a mountain, but it is very easy to roll down. Even if you were dead you could roll downhill. Now, the question is, are we dead corpses or are we living people? If you are living, you should not roll, but you should climb. Do not ever think that the work in the United States is easy. To me that mountain is steeper than the mountain in Taiwan. It even became so difficult that we had to resort to a lawsuit, to "appeal to Caesar." Praise the Lord, that mountain is about to be climbed over. Thus, the mountain in Taiwan is not so steep. Do not be discouraged by my words. My saying that this would be hard work is a word of guidance. Do not regard it as easy. The easiest among the six items is to go to the campus. There on the campus, you are not only running on a plain, you are even running down a slight slope. It is very easy to "drive your car" there. Once you start to drive, you will certainly reach the goal. Those who work on the campus should not say that they have achieved something. This kind of achievement can be done by anyone.

John Wanting People to Repent and Change Their Concept

What is the difficulty with the home meetings? In order to have good home meetings, the concepts of all the brothers and sisters must be changed. To repent, to turn, was the word proclaimed by John the Baptist at the beginning of the New Testament. To repent is to have a turn in your mind, to change your concept.

The first sent one in the New Testament age was John the Baptist. His opening word was, "Repent" (Matt. 3:2). By this he was saying, "All your old Jewish concepts must be changed. You see that my father, Zechariah, is the leading priest, taking the lead to serve God by offering sacrifices, burning the incense, wearing the priestly robe, and eating the priestly food. Although I am his son, I wear camel's hair and eat locusts and wild honey. I forsook the temple, and I would not offer sacrifices or burn incense. I am here to make you change your concept. Throw away the old things!" Jesus Christ brought in a new beginning.

Today we cannot deny that the church in Taipei, with thirty-six years of history, has also grown old. Not only Taipei, but the entire island of Taiwan and the entire Lord's recovery have also become old. The Lord's recovery began in 1922. The first church was established in Foochow, sixty-three years ago. But now we have become old. We fought and struggled most vigorously around 1930, because it was not an easy thing to have the Lord's recovery in China. At that time a completely new recovery was brought in. Then the recovery went to Taiwan. But gradually, the situation among us has become one of oldness.

The Lord Jesus Also Wanting People to Repent and Change Their Concept

John came and cried, "Repent." Following him, the Lord Jesus also said, "Repent." (Matt. 4:17). To repent means to change your concept. When the Lord sent out the seventy disciples they also preached that people should repent (Luke 10:9-11). On the day of Pentecost, when the Holy Spirit descended, Peter rose up and also spoke the same word. The Jews asked him, "What should we do?" Peter said, "Repent and be baptized, each one of you, upon the name of Jesus Christ" (Acts 2:38). To be baptized means to bury all your oldness. Bury all the Judaistic means to bury all your oldness. Bury all the Judaic doctrines, the old Jewish traditions, the law, and the Mosaic Old Testament. In this way the church was completely new from the very beginning.

THE HOME MEETINGS BEING THE FOUNDATION OF THE CHURCH MEETINGS

The topic of this message is "The Foundation of the Church Meetings." In anything you do, there is always a foundation. Even language itself has a foundation. The

twenty-six letters of the English alphabet are the foundation of the English language. What is the foundation of the
church meetings? It is not hard for you to find out from
Acts how the three thousand and five thousand met after
they got saved. They met in the temple and from house to
house, from one home to another. When they were in the
temple, it was mainly Peter and John who spoke. If you
were to ask the Apostles Peter and John to visit the three
thousand and the five thousand saved ones, who com-
prised at least a few thousand homes, even if they wore out
the soles of their feet they still could not reach every one of
them.

Acts chapter five also says, "And every day, in the
temple and from house to house, they did not cease
teaching and bringing the good news of Jesus as the
Christ." There were absolutely no different teachings at
that time. Those who were saved, even though they were
saved for only a day or two, began to meet in their homes.
They definitely did not speak the teachings of Moses, nor
did they speak the doctrines of Isaiah. Every household
was speaking what they had personally heard from Peter's
speaking in the temple.

The home meetings were the foundation of the church
meetings. The big meetings in the temple were not the
foundation. Once the big meetings in the temple ended,
they were over. In the big meetings believers were produced,
and they were then brought to individual home meetings.
The church meetings were not built up in the big meetings
in the temple, but rather, the church meetings were built up
in every house, from house to house.

Acts chapter eight says that a great persecution arose
in Jerusalem not too long after the three thousand and the
five thousand were saved. They all left Jerusalem; only the
twelve apostles remained there. From this we see that the
propagation of the Lord's gospel and the spreading of the
testimony of the Lord's church did not depend primarily on
the apostles, but rather on those who were dispersed. They
brought people to salvation everywhere they went. I can
guarantee that no big meetings existed then. The big

meetings are not the foundation of the church. The meetings from house to house, the meetings in the homes, are the foundation of the church. The big meetings are a kind of skating on ice. It is the home meetings that can actually keep people. This light is very clear in the Bible.

The Home Meetings Starting in Taiwan

We saw this from the beginning. Thus, we encouraged migration fifty or sixty years ago. However, it was very difficult to bring people to salvation during those days in mainland China, and there were no big meetings at all to rely upon. To have five people baptized was an earth-shaking event. In the eighteen years from 1922 to 1940, no more than thirty-seven people were baptized at one time. In 1940 the church in Chefoo saw the light concerning the church preaching the gospel. From that time on, a hundred or more were baptized each time. It was because of the increase in number that there was the need to meet in homes, but we did not go to the extent of meeting in small groups. The small group meetings did not come into being until we arrived in Taiwan.

In Taipei, we first began to meet in the old hall. When we gained more people, we met in several areas. When even more were added, we divided them into the homes. These home meetings brought in tens of thousands of people. The churches on the whole island of Taiwan increased from four or five hundred to forty or fifty thousand in the period from 1949 to 1957. However, in 1958 we got distracted and started to go downhill. The downward slope was not a steep one, but rather gentle. We have been walking downhill since 1958, for twenty-seven years.

When we first escaped from the big meetings in the denominations to climb this mountain, we climbed to the home meetings. But before we could reach the peak, we were distracted and could not climb any further, and instead went downhill. We went downhill to such an extent that we paid attention to big meetings and eloquent speakers. Whoever can speak attracts people. The saints have acquired a habit of listening to sermons. Before going

to a meeting, they first ask who the speaker is. If Paul is
speaking, everybody goes. If Mark is speaking, they say, "I
don't have the time to go." Thus, the foundation of the
church is no longer the homes, but the preachers and the
big meetings. This is nothing but fallen Christianity.

The Bible Stressing Mutual Fellowship

In Christianity there is little emphasis on home
meetings or small group meetings. Mostly they have a congregation and each congregation hires a pastor. If this pastor has a doctoral degree, has some capability, sociableness,
and eloquence, and if when he opens his mouth, he can
speak of both the past and the present and both the East
and the West, then his congregation will certainly flourish
and prosper. When a big preacher comes, tens of thousands
may come to listen to the sermon. When the big preacher
leaves, everyone leaves also. Everyone is skating on ice,
and because the ice is thin, it melts to water when the big
preacher leaves.

Why do people hold revival meetings in Christianity? It
is because they are deflated. To hold a revival meeting is
like giving a heart-strengthening injection. The foundation
of Christianity is not in the home meetings, but in their big
meetings. Those churchgoers in the same denominational
church may never have talked to one another. When I was
small, I went with my mother to a Sunday service for
nearly twenty years. I never talked to anyone; neither did
anyone talk to my mother. Everyone was dressed up on
Sunday for church, sitting quietly in the pew. When we
raised our heads, the first thing we saw was the hymn
numbers posted on the board, so we knew which hymns
were to be sung that morning. Someone would then call out
these hymns. After the singing, someone would preach the
sermon and then someone would make announcements
about certain things. Finally, there was the benediction on
the congregation. After the benediction, we all got up. I did
not say anything to anyone, nor did anyone speak to me,
but we simply went our own ways. Where were the mutual

fellowship and communication, and the steadfast continuing in the teaching of the apostles, as recorded in the
Bible?

The condition of fallen Christianity is that it relies on
big meetings, on human capability, and on eloquent
speakers. Sixty years ago, the Lord showed us that the
truth of the Bible was not to take this way, but rather to
emphasize mutual fellowship. How can a ten thousand
member church have mutual fellowship? If the way is
through big meetings, then it is not easy to talk once to
every member, even after meeting for ten years. But if
people come into a home, they have to speak even though
they normally do not speak much, and their situation will
be made clear through this kind of speaking. You may
even be able to discover what kind of sickness they have
through your speaking. The home meetings are the
foundation of the church.

THE BUILDING UP OF THE CHURCH DEPENDING UPON HOME MEETINGS TO LAY ITS FOUNDATION

Last winter I read a book entitled *The Pilings* which
was written by a Chinese Catholic priest. It mentioned
that for the church to be built up, it must use pilings for its
foundation in order to be stable. The pilings are the home
meetings. As an example to illustrate his point, he said
that the church assembly hall in Taiwan practiced home
meetings and that they did the best in driving pilings.

In recent years we put much emphasis on the big
meetings. When we saw the number decreasing, we
changed our way of speaking. When we saw that people
disliked what they were hearing, we changed to another
topic. Whether we did it this way or that way, we were only
concerned with the speaker. However, we did not really
know how to use our family treasure—the home meetings.
We went back to depending on big meetings and following
the way of Christianity. This is my burden tonight: we
must change our concept. The big meetings have their
usefulness, but the people of the entire world are "on the
ice." We want to lead some of them to skate to the "land"

and keep them in the home meetings. Only in this way can the church survive.

According to my several decades of experience, I know that when the home meetings were set up, at the beginning those who had not been meeting just came back to meet and give testimonies. This made everyone happy. After the second or third week had passed, what else could we speak? Serving a dessert again and again made it lose its taste. Why did these meetings not last long? Because there was no content. By now you have already experienced this taste. While I was in the United States, I received a letter from some brothers in Taipei that said, "The situation of the home meetings in Taipei is one-third up, one-third down, and one-third breaking even." In accounting terms, the credit side was the same as the debit side, that is, it was a wasted effort. This is because everyone has the concept that we still depend on the big meetings. You are still hoping to have a capable speaker to come and preach to you.

Bringing Christ as the Content
to the Home Meetings

For the home meetings to last, we must bring Christ. Only Christ will not wither; only Christ will not wane. There is a famous hymn in Christianity that goes, "Beautiful flowers will wither and the full moon will wane; only my best friend will never depart." The best friend is the Lord Jesus. Perhaps you may say that your home meeting has not waned, nor has it withered, but I am afraid that over half of our home meetings are already like a night-blooming flower; midnight has passed and they have started to droop. Tonight I want to proclaim the word of John the Baptist—"Repent!" To repent means to change your concept. You must change your concept. Do not emphasize the big meetings. As a minimum, you must consider the home meetings to be on the same level as the big meetings.

The Big Meeting Hall Having Many Uses

I admit that the big meetings have their use and are necessary. We are now actively looking for land to build a big meeting hall. I can guarantee that the Lord will surely lead us to success. As soon as the big hall is completed, within half a year you will see its uses. Do we not want to evangelize Taiwan? At least five hundred new co-workers should be raised up each year. These young brothers and sisters need to be trained, and the training requires a place for them to live. On this land there will be not only a meeting hall, but also a place for activities which may serve as a weekend camp. The twenty-one halls of Taipei are twenty-one units. There are also almost twenty satellite churches surrounding Taipei. When both are added together, there are forty units, and each unit may use this facility for a week. Furthermore, the campus work of the churches in each locality will also be able to use it.

Our gospel must spread to the homes, cities, and villages. However, to really gain the good material, we need to go to the young students. Therefore, we need to work on the campuses. Based on our past experience, the most effective way to work on the campuses is through the summer and winter camps. We go to a campus to contact some gospel friends. When the weekend comes, we do not go to movies or dancing parties. We only go to look for gospel friends. Then we may tell them, "Our church has a mountain camp with a garden and dormitories. Let us go and stay there for a day." If you bring them up to the mountain to have a walk together and a little talk, they will surely be saved.

We will build a baptismal on the mountain, so that people can be baptized as soon as they get saved. Every week we will bring people in groups up to the mountain. Out of the ten we bring up the mountain, even though not all ten will be baptized, at least there could be seven or eight. This is what has been on my heart. It is surely worth promoting. Those of you who are at least somewhat involved in the campus work all know that this is the most effective way. Especially today in Taiwan, when the weekend comes, the students do not like to stay on the campus. They will surely go out to travel. The best place is to go up to the mountain. The big meeting hall does have its uses, but if we simply do this kind of work and have no foundation, then we will still use the ice-skating way, and many will skate away. Just as they skate in, they will skate out.

Only the Home Meetings Being Able to Keep People

When it comes to God's work, the beginning is always the best. After it is handed over to man, it begins to go downhill. The beginning of Acts was the best. There was the "skating rink" in the big meetings to skate people in. Many skated in. Then there were the meetings from house to house to bring people into the foundation of the church. Once a person joined the home meetings, he was kept. This is God's wisdom.

The churches in the Lord's recovery on the five continents number about six hundred fifty in total. Particularly in Central and South America, the rate of increase has been very fast, and it is still increasing. My work in the United States is very busy, yet I had to come back to lead Taipei, to lay a good foundation here, because this is the model. If the source here is not clear, the work cannot be spread elsewhere. Thus, I beg you all to pick up the burden to pray and to strive together. Do not belittle the home meetings. Whether we can succeed, whether the Lord can work out a way among us, all depends on our effort now. Otherwise, the Lord will have to look for some other people, and we will go downhill, becoming yet another group in Christianity.

DAILY LABORING DOUBLE ON CHRIST

Brothers and sisters, when you come to the meeting, do you expect to hear a capable speaker? Your concept of relying on capable speakers must be turned. This is the first thing I want to do tonight. What should we do after we all have turned our concept? We all have had experiences of having our concepts turned. At the moment he is saved, everyone has his concept turned. Then we had to learn to pray, read the Word, know the truth, grow in life, experience Christ, gain Christ, and enjoy the riches of Christ. Christ is our good land of Canaan. When we labor on Him, daily working on Christ, we shall reap a harvest.

God's way of working is always balanced. You see that a man has two hands and two shoulders. The left side is the big meetings and the right side is the home meetings; thus the big meetings and the home meetings are balanced. After we are balanced, we need to double our prayer, double our reading of the Bible and our seeing of light from the Bible, and double our experience of Christ.

The Home Meetings Being the Way to Achieve the Building Up

In the church, all the brothers and sisters love the Lord. It is based upon your love of the Lord that I have the burden to lead you. Since you love the Lord, you must mean business with Him. Your love for the Lord should not be vain talk. Do you love the Lord? Let me tell you, the Bible tells us that the Lord has only one way to build His church, to reach His goal. This way is the home meetings. This is something that the big meetings cannot accomplish. The big meetings in Christianity are like the age of the judges. The age of the judges depended entirely upon a spiritual giant. When a Samson rose up, it was good. When he died, Israel was through. The age of the judges of the Old Testament prefigured today's Christianity. If we only pay attention to big meetings and neglect the home meetings, we are reenacting the story of the age of the judges. We must have our concept turned. We do not want judges; we want homes. Every home must be strong, and to have a strong home, you must first be strong.

It is preferable for the home meetings to have not more than twelve people. Five or six is the best. Seven or eight is also good. Eight or ten is fine. Because we love Him and mean business with Him, we pray daily, read the Word, learn the truth, see the light, experience Christ daily, and labor on Christ. When we come together, the eight or ten of us all have experiences to share. Then spontaneously we

will not just come to be a part of an audience depending on
others to speak. Last night I met a Dutch brother. He spoke
Chinese very well. He told me that he can speak Dutch and
that he has also learned German, French, English, and
Chinese. He knows five languages. Today, is it easier for
you to follow Christ, experience Christ, enjoy Christ, or for
a Dutch man like him to learn Chinese? He can turn his
Dutch tongue into a Chinese tongue and speak Chinese.
Why can we not turn our tongue into a "Christ tongue"? It is
because we are not willing. We love the Lord, and every
day we carry our Bible bags and rush to the meetings. Let
us not just bring our Bible bags. Please read the Bible, and
learn to speak the word of Christ. Then you will have
experiences to bring to the meetings and the meetings will
be rich.

The Spirit in Acts is the speaking Spirit. He speaks
continuously. If everyone in a meeting rushes to speak
first, if one has not finished speaking and another wishes
he would quickly finish speaking, would that meeting not be
rich? With meetings like this time after time, everyone's
taste for depending on the big meetings will be changed.
The ones who were just brought in and the ones who have
not been meeting for a long time will no longer be
concerned with the big meetings, and they will feel that the
small meetings are also very good. A church meeting like
this will have turned from building on the wrong foundation to building on the right foundation. Only a church
like this is worthy of praise. It does not matter whether the
capable speaker will come today or not; we can meet by
ourselves. This church then has a foundation.

The church in Taipei is both big and stable, yet it may
not be reliable. If the concept here is turned to the point
that, even if the so-called capable speakers do not come for
ten years, the church still flourishes and progresses,
then we will have succeeded. We should preach the gospel
and lead the brothers and sisters to stand firm, so that
everyone is a soldier and our army is everywhere. In this
way the church will be stable. At that point we will really
be able to evangelize Taiwan. If we continue to depend on

big meetings and cannot even evangelize ourselves, how can we evangelize Taiwan? If your small family has not been evangelized and your relatives have not been evangelized, it is impossible to evangelize Taiwan. We need the Holy Spirit to initiate the work so that even a newly saved one can speak. Every family speaks. Everyone speaks. Every saved one is a preacher.

Experiencing Christ and Overflowing with Christ

I hope that everyone's concept will be changed. Only after our concept is changed will these things follow: intensifying our prayer and reading the Bible; intensifying our fellowship with the Lord; intensifying our pursuit of light, truth, and seeing the vision; growing in life to follow the Lord; enjoying Christ; and gaining Christ. If you have all these, you will have something to say in any meeting you attend. In your home meetings now, there is some giving of testimonies and some calling of hymns, but this is mostly done in a natural way. Some of these things have become a regulation. Both the natural way and the way of regulation are not right. What is right? You must stay home to pray more, read the Bible more, fellowship with the Lord more, have more experience of life, and seek more light and truth. If you are like this every day, when you stand up to speak, what you say will not be natural or by way of regulation. You will have so many riches that you will overflow. This matter of overflowing is the following of the Spirit. Formerly, I did not know what it meant to be carried along by the Spirit. Now I am clear. You pray, read the Bible, experience the Lord, and you are filled with the Lord within. Then wherever you go, the Holy Spirit carries you along. When you are full and come to the home meeting, your speaking will not be according to the natural way; neither will it be by way of regulation. Rather, it will be the outflow of the Lord's riches. You overflow, and I overflow. This home meeting will then be rich. In the home meetings we speak in everyday language. Everyone can speak this language. Whatever you hear in your daily life, you speak. You do not need to put on a show or to pretend;

you simply overflow naturally and spontaneously. The
foundation of the church is not with the long sermons of
the apostles, but with the homes. You give a testimony,
and I speak a word of enlightenment. If everyone speaks,
this will add up to an abundance. Seeing and hearing this,
the newcomers and the newly recovered ones will all
receive the profit. In this way the foundation of the church
will be solid and the church will last.

THE SIX COMMISSIONS OF THE HOME MEETINGS

The first thing we must do is change our concept. The
home meetings are not merely a method. From now on we
will neither uplift the big meetings nor despise them. We
will regard the big meetings and the home meetings
equally. According to today's situation, you should not
consider that to recover someone, you must bring that
person to the big meetings in order to be successful. Of
course that is very good, but you should not require this.
As long as he can come to the home meetings every week,
that will be very good. First, lay this foundation in him.
Second, the home meetings should strive to recover those
who have not been meeting for a long time. In Taipei, there
are tens of thousands of brothers and sisters who have
not been meeting. The three to five thousand of you who
are meeting regularly must all be in the home meetings to
recover those who have not been meeting for a long time.
Third, preach the gospel widely. The home gospel must go
out from the homes. Even the campus work can go out
from the homes. The homes are the foundation. If the
homes are not strong and even you yourself need shepherding, then who can shepherd? If the home meetings are
not strong, even the children's work cannot be done. For a
nation to be strong, the homes must be strong. For a
church to be strong, the home meetings must be built up.
The homes are the foundation, the base, of all activities.
Fourth, keep the people. The home meetings must keep and
uphold people and even cause people to want to come back.
You have to work on the home meetings to such an extent
that they have the power to attract and keep people. Fifth,

you need to strengthen the riches in the home meetings. The content of the home meetings must be rich. Sixth, when the home meetings become so rich, the highest goal of expressing Christ will be attained.

The home meetings are not easy to build up. This is a great and high mountain which is not easy to climb. Beginning with changing our concept, then recovering those who have not been meeting for a long time, widely preaching the gospel, upholding, strengthening and enriching the content of the meetings, we will finally reach God's highest goal for the church—expressing Christ. May the Lord have mercy on us. May we all pray for this matter.

CHAPTER TWO

THE CONTENTS OF THE HOME MEETINGS

(1)

Scripture Reading: Acts 2:22-24, 32-33, 36-38, 41-42; 5:42; 1 Cor. 2:2; 14:23a, 26; 1 Tim. 1:3-4

CONTINUING IN THE TEACHING OF THE APOSTLES

In this message we will continue to speak on home meetings. This item is the most difficult one to work out among the six spiritual works. When Peter initiated the church meetings, it was under the direct working of God. What is worked out by God is the highest. The highest standard was daily to have big meetings in the temple and small gatherings in the homes. With Peter in the beginning in Acts 2 and 5, the church meetings consisted of both big meetings and small gatherings. The big meetings were held in the temple, while the small gatherings were from house to house. Whatever was spoken and taught in the big meetings—was it left unspoken, or was it changed, in the small meetings? Certainly not. What was spoken in the small getherings was the continuation of what was spoken in the big meetings.

In the Chinese translation, the meaning of Acts 2:42, "With endurance they kept the teaching of the apostles, the communicating with one another, the breaking of bread, and prayers," is completely changed because in the original, the main verb is "to continue," and in Greek "with endurance" actually means "steadfastly." This verse has everything to do with home meetings and with all matters related to the meetings. At the present time, I feel it is best to translate this verse: "And they were continuing steadfastly in the teaching and the fellowship of the apostles, in the breaking of bread and the prayers." Under the ministry of Peter, the meetings of the church began and remained steadfastly in the teaching and the fellowship of the apostles and in the breaking of bread and prayers. These were the typical contents of the early church meetings.

SPEAKING ONLY CHRIST BEING THE FOUNDATION OF THE CONTENTS OF THE CHURCH MEETINGS

Acts 5:42 says, "And every day, in the temple and from house to house, they did not cease teaching...." What were they teaching? Acts 2:42 says, "And they were continuing steadfastly in the teaching ... of the apostles." Therefore, their teaching must have been the teaching of the apostles. After reading Acts 2:22-24, 32-33, and 36-38 you will realize that what they were preaching was the first message given by Peter, a message in which Peter spoke only of Christ. This message set the foundation of the contents of the church meetings. When the church was first established, the believers preached only of Christ's incarnation, His human living on the earth, His being persecuted, His being crucified, and His entering into the suffering of death, and of God's raising Him from the dead, exalting Him into the heavenlies, and making Him both Lord and Christ, whereupon He poured out the all-inclusive Spirit. These are the contents of the church meetings and the basic principle of the church meetings, which principle is just Christ.

After hearing this first message, the multitude was pierced in their hearts and asked the apostles and brothers, saying, "What should we do, men, brothers?" Peter said, "Repent and be baptized, each one of you, upon the name of Jesus Christ." All those who heard believed, repented, and were baptized. The three thousand believers then continued steadfastly in the teaching which they had heard when they were saved. For generations the Jews had been preaching Moses, the Ten Commandments, offerings, gifts, worshipping God in the temple, and burning incense. Now, suddenly, upon hearing Peter speak, "Men, Israelites, hear these words: Jesus Christ, a man demonstrated by

God by works of power and wonders and signs, you nailed to the cross and killed. But God raised Him up, having loosed the pangs of death, exalted Him to the right hand of God, made Him both Lord and Christ, and caused Him to pour out the all-inclusive Spirit," they simply received this teaching. They were saved and continued steadfastly in this teaching. This teaching became the contents of the church meetings.

Peter spoke this teaching in the temple, in the big congregation. Three thousand newly saved ones continued in this teaching, not in the big meetings but from house to house. What was spoken in the big meetings was continued in the small gatherings. This was the practice. What Peter had spoken in the big meetings was repeated again and again in the small gatherings from house to house, where they daily spoke of Jesus Christ. Among the three thousand who were baptized, there must have been at least five hundred households. If Peter with his Bible were the only one who must go and speak from house to house, even if he totally exhausted himself, he still would not have been able to visit all of the houses. The practice in that day was that what Peter spoke the first day was taken back and repeated from house to house the following day. It may seem that this was not possible, yet this is definitely recorded in the Bible.

PAUL PREACHING ONLY JESUS CHRIST
AND THIS ONE CRUCIFIED

At the end of January 1985 I flew back to the United States from Taipei. As soon as the plane took off, I already knew that the home meetings would develop to the present stage. At first the home meetings recovered some who had not been meeting for a long time. Those who had not met for twenty or thirty years came back to the meetings. How dear it was when they all came together, and how sweet it was to sing,

> "Blest be the tie that binds
>   Our hearts in Christian love....
> And perfect love and oneness reign
>   Through all eternity."   *Hymns, #860*

If an old sister who had not been meeting for twenty years had sung this song, she would surely have burst into tears, and everyone else with her. However, beautiful flowers fade, a full moon wanes, and good things do not last. The meeting was good the first time, the second time, the third time, but by the fourth time it had become tasteless. And by the fifth time old wives' fables had begun.

When the church began to meet, the way begun by Peter was continued by Paul. How do we know this? In 1 Corinthians 2:1-2 Paul says, "When I came to you, brothers ... I determined not to know anything among you except Jesus Christ, and this One crucified." This tells us that Paul preached only one subject in the church at Corinth, that is, Jesus Christ and this One crucified. He did not speak about ethics, morality, philosophy, law, or Old Testament doctrines. What he spoke and preached was Jesus Christ and this One crucified.

BIG MEETINGS BEING FOR EXHIBITING CHRIST, AND EACH ONE HAVING SOMETHING TO BRING

In chapter fourteen of the same Epistle Paul talks about the Christian meeting. When he speaks of the whole church being together in one place, he first speaks of the big meetings. What should be done in the big meetings? In verse 26, Paul says: "Whenever you come together, each one has a psalm, has a teaching, has a revelation ...." The word "has" in this verse does not indicate to have in the future but to have in the present. When you come to a meeting, before leaving home you already have a psalm or a revelation; therefore, you bring them to the meeting. Before the meeting you already have something. It is not that you have nothing before the meeting, yet you bring your Bible and come empty-handed, thinking that because you have had a terrible week, you have nothing, but are assured that in the meeting you will receive grace. Thus you sit in your seat and wait for grace. When the meeting begins or the Holy Spirit moves within, you are inspired, and so you choose a hymn. No, it is that before you leave for the meeting, you are one who already "has," as described by a hymn: "Whene'er we meet with Christ endued...and thus exhibit Christ" *(Hymns, # 864)*. This hymn was written according to the types of the Old Testament feasts. Each year the Israelites brought the produce of the land to the feasts. They brought cattle, sheep, grain, and new wine. They brought the produce of the good land and then exhibited all these riches. All the produce typifies Christ. The riches of the produce that they brought to the feast typifies the Christ brought to the New Testament meetings. Our meetings should be an exhibition of Christ.

The big meetings spoken of by Paul are those to which each one brings Christ. However, our big meetings are not like this. We are somewhat like Christianity, with one man speaking and the rest listening. In Paul's ministry there were not only big meetings but also home meetings. We know this because in his Epistles he mentions the church in the home of a certain brother at least four times (Rom. 16:5; 1 Cor. 16:19; Col. 4:15; Philem. 2). If the church was in a brother's home, there certainly must have been home meetings. From this you can see that there were big meetings and home meetings under the ministries of both Peter and Paul.

HOME MEETINGS BEING LIKE THE ARK OF GOD, REQUIRING EVERYONE'S SHOULDER

Big meetings allow people to slip in, but after not too long people also slip out. Why do big meetings have difficulty keeping people? Because there is not the fundamental level of the home meetings to hold them. I hope that you brothers and sisters who love the Lord can all see this. Otherwise, the Lord will have no way. If we only emphasize the big meetings and neglect the home meetings, we will let the Lord down. We who love the Lord should not do such a thing. Please do not decide the future of the home meetings according to the present condition. Because of this very burden I came to Taiwan three times in less than three months. I know what the need is, and I also know where the difficulty is. I hope that the brothers

and sisters would all get into this burden. The home
meeting is like the ark of God, and it requires your
shoulder to help carry it. If you have the desire, please
accept this burden to participate in the home meetings to
enrich them. When you attend a home meeting, do not
strengthen the meeting according to the natural concept,
but rather strengthen and enrich it according to the types of
the Old Testament and according to the clear revelation in
the New Testament, in order that each home meeting may
prosper daily.

THE NEED TO LABOR ON CHRIST DAILY

What are the types in the Old Testament? What is the
revelation in the New Testament? They are for us to
fellowship with the Lord daily and to enjoy the Lord and
experience Him daily. This is a daily matter, not merely a
matter for one day. In the case of the Israelites, after every
family was allotted a piece of land, they had to first get rid
of all the weeds, chop down the trees, and clean out the
stones. Besides all this, they had to level the ground and
till it for the sowing of the seed. Then they had to work out
a way of irrigation. After the irrigation they had to weed
further and nurture their fields, staying busy daily for
about three to four months. Finally, the fields would be
filled with golden grains. At this time they still had to reap
the harvest and dry the grains in the field before storing
everything in the barns. However, these grains were still
too coarse to be brought to the feast, so they had to grind
them into flour and make them into cakes for their own
enjoyment as well as bring them to God as an offering for
God's enjoyment. The herdsmen also had to do the same.
Early every morning they had to take out the flock, and
every evening they had to bring it back into the fold. Then
when the great day of the feast came, they would be able to
bring a herd of cattle or a flock of sheep to the mount of
Jehovah to offer them up to the Lord one by one. Therefore
God told the people that they must come to worship Him
three times a year, but they should not appear before Him

empty (Deut. 16:16). This indicates that we should come together at appointed times and bring Christ with us; we must not come empty.

How could you not come empty? It all depends on your laboring on the good land. It all depends on how much you have labored. Do you fellowship with Him every morning, worshipping Him, praying to Him, reading His Word, and waiting in His presence? If you cannot do so for half an hour, I hope you can do it for at least fifteen minutes. If you labor daily, in due time, you will naturally be able to reap the harvest. The harvest is not for your own enjoyment, but for you to offer to God and to share with your fellow members in the presence of God. This is the Christian meeting.

AT THE FUNDAMENTAL LEVEL, THERE BEING NO NEED TO DEPEND ON BIG MEETINGS

When the Israelites met together, there were also priests who would speak to them. However, the fundamental level was not built on the priests' exposition of the Scriptures. The fundamental level was the households. Everyone brought his year-long accumulation of riches; this was the foundation of the big meetings. Today the foundation of our big meetings should be the brothers and sisters experiencing Christ daily and thus having the riches of Christ, and everyone bringing these riches with him when he comes to meet. The church is built upon such a fundamental level.

At this time, to have some gifted ones who have received revelation from the Lord to release some messages is also an urgent need of the church. We must see that there are two sides. In the case of the ancient Israelites, suppose each household were to bring the rich produce to the feasts. Then, even if most of the priests were dead, that would not have greatly affected their feasts because they already had the fundamental level which could not be shaken. Today in the church meetings, if everyone has experienced Christ and everyone has brought Christ to the meetings, then whether there is anyone among us who can give messages or not, that would not affect the foundation of our meetings.

Today our situation is like the Israelites coming empty. Your two hands are empty, and mine are also empty. You look at me and I look at you. We have nothing. What are we doing here? All the eloquent ones are gone. The fundamental level is gone. Let me repeat: the way of depending on a great evangelist does not work. People will swarm like bees to listen to the sermon, but when the evangelist is gone, the crowd also goes. As the swallows fly to the south, so they will return to the north. When I came this time, I was very clear that I did not want to have any big conferences. I am here only to speak about the condition of the church and to turn everyone's concept. After the turn, we must go back to the home meetings.

ONLY THE HOME MEETINGS BEING ABLE TO REACH GOD'S GOAL

This does not mean that once we go back to the home meetings we will drop all big meetings. Even the airplanes today cannot violate God's law of creation. They must depend on two wings to fly. The big meetings are one wing and the home meetings are another wing. Both wings are needed. However, in the long run the small gatherings are more dependable than the big ones.

Dear brothers, truly from my spirit I am asking you—I am actually begging you—to receive the Lord's leading today. If you do not believe my words, you can wait and see. If we cannot follow the Lord, then He will have to find others, just as He found us in the beginning. If we should go back to repeat the history of Christianity, then the Lord would say, "All right, that is enough. I must go to others." Big meetings definitely cannot reach God's goal. To reach God's goal we must depend on small gatherings.

Today is the scientific era. In everything we are all accustomed to specialization. When we are sick, we go to the doctor; when we are sued, we go to the lawyer; and when we need prayers, we go to the pastor. This is because only doctors know medicine, only lawyers know the law, and only pastors know how to pray. Such concepts as these are natural. The poison of Christianity has spread into us. Subconsciously, we also would like to have a specialist to preach to all of us. However, even sixty years ago I had already seen that the Lord called us out to go this way to be His testimony. This testimony is different from this age, and it is absolutely different from today's Christianity. The Lord's recovery is absolutely not just another work in Christianity.

Nevertheless, in Taipei, the birthplace of the Lord's recovery in Taiwan, in the past twenty-six or twenty-seven years the brothers have faithfully "kept the family property," which is to emphasize the big meetings without having the small gatherings. Even though everyone has been endeavoring to testify for the Lord, unconsciously we have been going downhill on a seemingly level road. Over twenty years this downward trend has made quite a difference. Now I beg everyone to change his concept, to turn his attention from the big meetings to the small gatherings. Try your best to do this. Dear brothers and sisters, there is no other way. If we depart from this, we can only go downhill and will be in the same stream as Christianity. We will be unable to keep the Lord's present testimony.

DOING OUR BEST TO BUILD UP THE HOME MEETINGS

If we are faithful to keep the Lord's present testimony, we must do our best to build up the home meetings. Do not think the home meetings cannot bring people into salvation. Let me tell you, in the eleven years after we moved to Anaheim, we had increase in the first three years, but in the last eight years, because of the rising up of the libelous ones, there were hardly any English-speaking ones brought in. Then, after the home meetings began in January 1985, within three months forty or fifty were added. All of these were not brought in through the big meetings but through the home meetings. Another discovery is that people brought in through the home meetings are remaining fruit.

People who slip in through the big meetings will also slip out at the end of the big meetings. Therefore, by comparison, the effort spent saving people in the home meetings is more dependable than that spent in the big meetings.

We do not plan to drop the big meetings. On the Lord's Day when everyone has a day off, we ought to use big meetings to preach the truth, spread the gospel, and seize the opportunity to propagate the work of the Lord. However, if we should totally depend on the big meetings as in the past, we would give up the future of the Lord's recovery.

From now on we must all turn and put our attention on the home meetings. This is the fundamental level of the church meetings. On this solid fundamental level we can expand. The big meetings are useful but not dependable, whereas the home meetings are dependable. I hope this kind of fellowship will get into you. I plead with you to receive this vision and revelation. Let us spare no effort, but with one heart work in coordination to strengthen and enrich the home meetings. Then the Lord will have a way. I know that if the Lord speaks these words into your being, then the blessing is upon us and the horizon is glorious and full of expectation!

CHAPTER THREE

THE PROFIT AND LOSS COMPARISON OF THE HOME MEETINGS AND BIG MEETINGS

Scripture Reading: Acts 2:46; 5:42; 1 Cor. 14:23b, 26

I originally intended to use only the first two nights to speak about the home meetings. But the more I speak the more burden I have. Tonight I will speak more on the comparison of the profit and loss of the home meetings and the big meetings. I feel that we should consult the methods of others and also reconsider our experiences in the past thirty-six years here in Taipei. I believe that by comparing these two kinds of meetings, we will receive much benefit.

PROPAGATING FROM ONE SPEAKING TO ALL SPEAKING

We must admit that God's wisdom surpasses all. God's works are created by Him and accomplished by Him and have no need of any improvement. On the day of Pentecost the Holy Spirit was poured out. As a result three thousand were saved. Immediately the church was established and began to meet.

Acts 2:46 says, "And day by day, continuing steadfastly with one accord in the temple and breaking bread from house to house." Furthermore, we see in verse 42 that they were continuing steadfastly in the teaching of the apostles. Here we see a clear picture that the church meetings include on the one hand the big meetings and on the other hand the small gatherings. The big meetings were in the temple and the small gatherings were from house to house. In the big meetings in the temple surely Peter spoke and others listened to his speaking. When it came to the meetings from house to house, there must have been a good number of people sharing what they had heard in the temple.

Verse 42 says, ". . . continuing steadfastly in the teaching . . . of the apostles," and verse 46 says, "breaking bread from house to house." These two verses are two little show windows through which you can see the contents inside. They met from house to house and everyone spoke. They did not speak of their own things but they continued steadfastly in the teaching of the apostles and spoke whatever Peter had spoken. Within one to two days one speaking brother, Peter, was propagated into hundreds of speaking brothers and sisters.

SPREADING OUT FOR THE PROPER GROWTH

No one can deny that the home meetings have recovered some people, but they also have a danger. The danger of the home meetings is that while the capable ones are holding back, those who speak nonsense will speak in the meetings. The result of this situation is that nobody enjoys the meetings. In my garden there was a piece of lawn where the old grass was not growing. The brothers came to replace it for me, and they threw pieces of new sod here and there. After two to three months, these pieces of new sod all spread out and green grass grew everywhere. In a few years the grass will have no place to grow. Then it will crowd itself out and it all will become old. From this matter I learned a lesson that the church is like this. In Taipei, at the beginning we "threw pieces of sod out," but we did not have the assurance, for example, that the small meeting in Mu Zha was a church. We dared not say that the one in Shi Lin was a church or that the one in Pei Tao was a church, fearing that they would all be scattered by this kind of throwing out. But history tells us that the piece in Mu Zha became a church, the piece in Shi Lin became a church, and the piece in Pei Tao also became a church. Originally we were extremely worried about the small number meeting in Yong Ho and expended much effort there. To our surprise, today Yong Ho is larger than hall one in Taipei. Brothers and sisters in Yong Ho, if you do not spread further you will become old.

Today in the church in Taipei there is too much old grass crowding there. In 1949 we met first in hall one. The following year meeting halls were built. Immediately after the subdivision the small groups were established, group after group. All these pieces of sod were scattered and they grew very fast. Later on we got distracted, and a group of young people were influenced. They began to have dissenting opinions. In these circumstances the Lord led me to the United States. Since I arrived in the United States in 1960, three hundred fifty churches have been raised up in North and South America, Europe, Africa, and Australia. Yet here in Asia we have degraded into the Christianity way of meeting, the way of emphasizing the big meetings. The meetings in homes and small groups were either put aside or disregarded. We hoped that the big meetings would be attractive and that the number attending the big meetings would increase. We gave message after message, expecting to raise up some capable speakers. But this way did not bring in many and retained even fewer people. After twenty-seven years of labor the actual number of those attending the meetings was lower than it was over twenty years ago. This is the history. In these twenty-seven years many were baptized but they were not retained.

ONE BEING ABLE TO SPEAK AS SOON AS HE IS SAVED

Looking back, from 1949 to 1957 there were many small groups and they retained people. Once we began to practice the small groups people were brought in. On the other hand, because there were not many capable speakers, the message delivery was not that strong. This is the weakness of the home meetings. Now let us compare the profit and loss. The advantage of the home meetings is that it is easy to bring people in and retain them. But if the contents are poor, this weakness can be remedied. In the United States there are many schools with thousands of students and many teachers. If you expect every teacher to be like Billy Graham, then there is no way for the schools to go on. It does not matter how capable Billy Graham is; he cannot compare to those thousands of teachers, each one teaching twenty-five students. This is more than enough. In this way the education will be successful.

The Lord's wisdom is great. From the beginning there were big meetings in the temple and small group meetings in the homes. This was a good start which developed a good habit and laid a good foundation. On the day of Pentecost, as soon as one got saved, right away he began to speak. But our concept is not like this. We wonder how a person who just got saved yesterday can begin to preach today. We cannot believe that this is possible. This kind of view and atmosphere kills people. Who does not know how to speak? Even the most stupid person is able to learn a language. After learning, he naturally will speak. On the spiritual side, once we are saved, we have the Spirit of the Lord, we pray, we read the Bible, we attend the meetings, and we listen to so many messages. Yet when it is our turn to speak, we say that we do not know how. This is how the habit of having the big meetings has damaged us. The big meetings have killed all the functions of the saints and deprived people of their rights.

An elderly person will become sick if he stops walking for a few days. But all the sicknesses will disappear when he practices walking a few thousand steps every day. If an elderly person can be recovered by exercise, how much more this will do to a young person! The reason you are not able to speak is because you do not speak. The big meetings have killed the people's opportunity to exercise. The reason that we all do not speak is that we do not know how to speak. But, as an old Chinese saying says, "Three stinky cobblers are better than one smart general." If we rely only on the speakers, no one will like to speak in the meetings. I do not believe that anyone will prepare anything before the meetings. Everyone will come in to the meetings with a mouth waiting to be fed. If you do not give your children the opportunity to practice speaking while they are little, and later on you blame them for not knowing how to speak, it is because their father talks too much. Every time the father opens his mouth he gives a lecture. This causes the children to become dumb. I would rather have the father speak less and let the children speak more. Very often the so-called capable gifts kill many other gifts.

THE INCREASE IN NUMBER INDICATING THE WELL-BEING OF THE CHURCH

Now we need to use our calm mind and quiet spirit to consider the actual situation. I am very concerned that in the past twenty-seven years the number in the church in Taipei has not increased but rather decreased. Every aspect of the church in Taipei is stable, and there is no excuse for not having any increase. In Taiwan civilization is highly developed, education is widespread, the economy is prosperous, and public safety is well maintained. All the conditions are met, yet there has been no increase. This must mean that we have missed the mark. I am like a businessman wanting to see whether there is any profit after closing the account. It does not matter how well you have done; a loss indicates that something is not right. People who open factories and shops count money, but in the church we count people. In the business world making money does not prove everything, but in the church the number of people means everything. Without adequate gospel preaching in the church there will be no increase in number; without proper shepherding the church will not retain people; without adequate building up the number still will not increase. Only when the number in the church increases does it prove that every aspect of the church is doing well. As long as the number decreases, it does not matter how much you say a certain aspect is doing well, it is still not doing well. If a person is healthy, yet he cannot give birth to a child, this kind of health is not real health. The statistics of the church are absolutely the statistics of the number of people.

A COURT FOR EVERYONE TO PRACTICE ON

We are not throwing away the big meetings. The big meetings in the temple and the small gatherings from house to house are equally important. When I first started the home meetings I mentioned that there were three hundred people meeting in a meeting hall. This is like putting three hundred players on one court, so that the majority cannot play the game. Now the home meetings have started, and now one meeting place has been distributed into more than twenty places. With each court having eight to ten players playing ball, all can be on the court to play the game. In the long run the way of all coming together onto one court to play ball makes everyone useless. Now there are twenty courts. Even those who do not know how to play have a court. Everyone needs to practice to play. Practice makes perfect.

BRINGING THE "HAS" FROM OUR DAILY LABORING TO THE MEETING

I remember very clearly that in 1933 when I first went to Shanghai, Brother Nee called the brothers together and said that until that very day our way of meeting had not been completely freed from degraded Christianity. We had not been brought back to what is spoken of in 1 Corinthians 14:26, "Whenever you come together, each one has a psalm, has a teaching, has a revelation . . . ." He said the word "has" in Greek does not mean that we are going to have or that we will have, but that we already have in our hands. He said that this "has" means that as you fellowship with the Lord day by day and read the Word of the Lord at home, you have the knowledge. Then after coming into the meeting you surely have something to speak.

Later I understood what Brother Nee had said about this point. This is just like the feast celebrated by the children of Israel. They brought the produce of the land and the bullocks and the sheep from their herds and their flocks. They labored all year and were able to bring something from their herds, their flocks, and their fields to the feast. Some brought their bullocks, some brought their sheep, some brought their new wine, some brought the produce. Everyone brought something. This is the normal situation. The meetings among us have not come up to this point. So we still need to endeavor.

At that time Brother Nee mentioned that we needed to set up a ladder so that our way of meeting could jump from degraded Christianity to 1 Corinthians 14:26. He started a brothers' meeting for the brothers and a sisters' meeting for the sisters. In the brothers' meeting there was no chairman or preacher, but they were to practice together 1 Corinthians 14:26. One had this, the other had that, and everyone brought whatever he had. Let me tell you, from the beginning until 1949 when we had the brothers' meeting in Taiwan, it was never successful. Indeed, the brothers came, yet they all came empty-handed and sat down. Yes, no single person was leading the meeting, but it was just you looking at me and I looking at you. No one had anything to say. Later someone suggested that we give testimonies. In the beginning there were a few testimonies. Gradually all the testimonies were exhausted. Everyone still sat there looking at each other. What kind of meeting is this?

When we could not get through in the brothers' meeting in Taiwan, we then realized that it was because we had never built up the habit of speaking in the meetings. A habit is accumulated from daily experiences. What has been handed down for years is this habit of one gifted person speaking and others listening. Through many years and months we have developed this habit of listening to someone preach. Among us we do not have the habit of speaking. When the home meetings began we all were not used to speaking. This gave the opportunity for those talkative ones to rise up and speak nonsense.

NO LONGER OBSERVING THE HOME MEETINGS OBJECTIVELY AS A SPECTATOR

Today, by the Lord's grace, we must study how to uplift the standard of the home meetings. I hope those who can supply others will no longer observe quietly and remain silent. I hope they would understand that this is their meeting, their court on which to play ball, and their place to function and minister. I hope that they would turn from objectively observing as a spectator to bearing the burden for the meeting. If this is done, the contents of the home meetings will be strengthened.

We need to build up the home meetings as the foundation of the church meetings. The life pulse of the church depends upon the home meetings. The destiny of the church also depends upon the home meetings. If the home meeting is successful, the church will be strong. It is just like a Chinese saying, that in order to have a strong society and a strong nation the homes must first be kept in good order. Keeping one's home in good order comes before ruling over the nation and bringing peace to the world. The same applies to the church. It is impossible to have strong church meetings if the home meetings of the saints are not strong. This will then force us to rely on the spiritual giants. When Gideon comes, the church becomes strong. When Gideon is gone the church becomes weak. Then a Samson comes, and the church has a revival. When Samson is gone the church is down again. That was the abnormal situation in the age of the judges. It should not be like this among us. We should not take the way of relying only on the spiritual giants to lead the meeting. We should make the home meeting strong in every house. We should all concentrate our effort to uplift the home meetings. Do not speak when you are not sure that your speaking is from the spirit or that it will supply Christ to others. Those who should not speak, do not speak. Those who are able to supply and able to bear the responsibilities should all speak. Then there will be no more guests, no more spectators, and no one who does not bear some burden in the meeting. In this way the home meetings will certainly become strong.

TURNING OUR ATTENTION TO FINDING A WAY OUT

Let me tell you a real case. The Southern Baptist Church is one of the largest denominations in the United States. Recently we saw a statistic from one of their publications. There are fourteen million on their membership list. The meeting attendance is twelve million. The reason that they are able to retain people is because their Sunday school is the best. They employ the principle of small classes in their Sunday school. They do not first come together in one place. They are first divided into classes, each class being about thirty to fifty people. They have more than a thousand people who write the material for their Sunday school. Their material has greatly improved. They speak about one Body and say that a saved one has two natures. Every Lord's Day they meet in small classes using the same material.

In one of the cities in Texas there are two Southern Baptist churches. Their environment is the same, and they began to meet at the same time. But because one emphasized the big meetings, that is, one speaking and others listening, and the other emphasized the Sunday school classes, after some period of time the attendance of the one that practiced the big meetings was one thousand; the other that emphasized the classes had over ten thousand. In the same city, two groups with these two lines of big meetings and small meetings started to meet at the same time, and they brought in two different results. If in the past fifteen years we had turned our attention to the home meetings and not stressed the big meetings, and if we had compared the profit and loss today, I fully believe that our number would have at least doubled. May the Lord have mercy on us. We need to pray for this matter to adjust the habit of relying on the gifted brothers. Everyone should function to bring out Christ, that the home meetings would not be low or empty. Nineteen eighty-five is our experimental year. Let us all go into the laboratory to work. I also will follow in to work. I believe we will find a way. We cannot rely on our thirty-year history, keeping the old things, and not be willing to go on. When our number is not increasing we need to wake up to find a way out, like a businessman when the business is not making money. Let us please pray for this together.

Chapter Four

THE CONTENTS OF THE HOME MEETINGS

(2)

The most difficult area with the home meetings is their contents. In the big meetings the main emphasis is on one speaker. If the speaker is rich, the contents of the big meetings are also rich. But in the home meetings there is no big speaker. Instead, those who come together are all "small potatoes". What content do these small potatoes have? If you want to see a spiritual giant, you have to go to the largest meetings. If a person were not a spiritual giant, how could he gather an audience of one hundred thousand? How could he maintain such a meeting? But as we know, not everyone can be a spiritual giant, just as not everyone can be the president of a country. In the human realm, not everyone can be the principal of a school or even a teacher. It is not easy to find one among ten who can really teach well. In the spiritual realm, there are many who are saved, tens of thousands, but they are all small potatoes. One can only find a few spiritual giants. In general, there are more small potatoes.

THE BUILDING UP OF THE CHURCH DEPENDING UPON THE ORDINARY BROTHERS AND SISTERS

Let us now look at this matter from the Bible. On the day of Pentecost three thousand people were saved. On another day five thousand were saved. They all were filled with the Holy Spirit, meeting from house to house. Were there many spiritual giants among those few thousand? According to the record in Acts, we see a man called Stephen. In Acts 7 there is a long message given by him. Then there was the evangelist, Philip, who had the experience of being caught away. However, in the Bible we cannot find one gospel message preached by him. In Acts there is also a record of one named Barnabas. But again in the Bible we cannot find a record of his preaching. After these three, we cannot find any other names. If there were outstanding ones among those eight thousand, they would not have been omitted by Luke, the author of Acts. The preaching of Peter, message after message, is recorded in the Bible. Even the lengthy messages of Paul are recorded. From this we can see that at that time, besides Stephen, Philip, and Barnabas, the believers were all more or less at the same level. They were all small potatoes.

By reading the Bible in this way, we discover that what the Bible does not record is more meaningful than what is recorded. The first time Paul went out to preach, he went out with Barnabas. But Barnabas did not preach. Whenever there was the occasion to preach, it was Paul who spoke. In the Bible there are prophets and teachers. Yet the prophets and teachers are not necessarily spiritual giants. If Barnabas were an outstanding preacher, then Luke certainly would have recorded that fact. Probably the preaching of Timothy was also average, for among the twenty-seven books of the New Testament, not one was written by Barnabas or Timothy. Only Paul was a real spiritual giant. Among the twenty-seven books, he alone wrote fourteen of them. Here I want to point out to you all that for the church to be built up, it must be general, and it must depend on the small potatoes.

THE CHURCH BEING GOD'S FARM, WITH EVERYONE GROWING TOGETHER

The strength or weakness of a local church does not depend on spiritual giants, but on each small brother or sister. The Bible likens the church to a cultivated field, the farm of God (1 Cor. 3:9). A field planted with grains of wheat will be full of golden grain at harvest time. The field will be all even, just as if it had been cut by a barber. There will be no exceptionally high ones, nor any exceptionally low ones, but all will be the same height. The church is God's growing crop. The normal ones are all on the same level. It is the extraordinary ones who are abnormal. But our view is not like this. When we go to visit the churches, we always look at the few outstanding ones. If there are a few outstanding ones in a certain church, that church appears promising to us.

Based on my fifty years of observation and from my experience, I know that wherever there are outstanding ones, eventually that local church will have problems. Those local churches with ordinary believers are the ones which go on steadily. Those churches which depend upon able speakers are in a good condition for a short time, like the blossoming of the night-blooming flower, which does not last long. Their good condition does not last because the spiritual giant does not live very long. Moses said that the days of our lives are eighty years if we are strong. Even if a man lives to be eighty, the span of his life is only a handbreadth. After the spiritual giant has passed away, it is all over. But with the small potatoes, one generation follows another. Those born of the small potatoes are all small potatoes. They go on for generations. Paul has passed away. In these two thousand years, many would have liked to listen to Paul's preaching, but he passed away. There is not a second Paul on the earth. Yet there are many small potatoes. Those whom the Lord has saved on the earth are all small potatoes. We must change our concept. God has no intention to use spiritual giants to build the church.

In Ephesians 4 there are apostles, prophets, evangelists, shepherds and teachers (v. 11). But they are not the ones who build the church directly. Those who build the church directly are all small potatoes, which are all the members (v. 16). All the members of the Body hold Christ in love and grow because of Him. Those apostles, prophets, and gifted persons do not build the church directly. They can only be counted as middlemen. For a local church to be built up, it must rely on a group of ordinary people. They are all average persons with nothing outstanding about them. The more ordinary the saints are, the more normal the church will be, and the longer its good spiritual condition will last. The principle in the Bible is that God uses gifted persons to save people. Then, after the people are brought in, God uses all the saints to build the church directly. Therefore the Bible speaks of the meetings that are from house to house. The church must have home meetings.

TO ATTEND THE HOME MEETINGS
BEING TO EAT ORDINARY HOME COOKING

The attendants of a home meeting are all small potatoes. Therefore, we cannot expect them to have a very high content. But I would like to say that the most healthy food is the ordinary home cooking. If we eat a big feast every day, our life expectancy will not be long. Our home meeting should not be a feast, but it should be ordinary cooking. We hope that the home meetings will supply to us the ordinary home cooking. The problem today is that the home meetings only offer dessert, with no ordinary home cooking. It is not good to eat too much dessert. Too many sweets easily cause an excess of stomach acid. If one wants to be healthy, he has to eat food with less grease, sugar, and salt. If one takes care of these few things, the entire family will be healthy. A few months ago, when we just began to promote the home meetings, the testimonies we heard were as pleasant as eating ice cream. Brothers and sisters who had not been to a meeting for thirty years returned. How encouraging it was to hear testimonies like this. At that time, I worried that if the home meetings would not eat the ordinary home cooking, one day even the ice cream would be gone.

We have spent three evenings here to change our concept and to understand the real situation. Do not set your hope on the big meetings. This way is a dead end. Big meetings are all like skating on the ice. On the day that Peter preached the gospel, three thousand skated in. Then Paul preached the gospel everywhere, full of power, and many people skated in. But this cannot keep people. Today, degraded Christianity emphasizes big meetings and sets up seminaries to train preachers. But what the Bible shows us is planting (1 Cor. 3:6). The church is raising up small potatoes. We must change our concept. If we cannot prepare a big feast, that is all right. But we have to do some ordinary home cooking. If we are willing, many of us can prepare an ordinary home-cooked meal. Brothers and sisters, all of us love the Lord, and all of us hope that the church would be built up. Therefore, I believe you are all willing to receive this leading of the Lord.

Today on five continents there are more than six hundred churches. Every church has its eyes on the church in Taipei, because Taipei was the origination of the overseas churches. Therefore, the church in Taipei must be built up. We all must come back to the Bible, to pay attention to the building up of the home meetings according to the revelation and principle of the Bible, and to nurture the several thousand brothers and sisters in Taipei in the home meetings. Every home gathering is like a garden. Let us go and nurture the green and tender trees. We will surely succeed! Brothers and sisters, for the going on of the home meetings, let us bear the burden together. The home meeting is just like a family with eight or ten members. In such a family, one person alone does not prepare the meal, but everyone must cook. Even if you do not know how to cook, you have to go shopping and prepare meals at home that the whole family may eat and be healthy.

USING THE WORD SKILLFULLY TO UPLIFT THE CONTENTS OF THE HOME MEETINGS

How can we uplift and strengthen the content of the home meetings? And how can we enrich the content of the home meetings? We have to learn to use the Lord's Word skillfully. Christians who go to the Sunday morning service also read the Bible. But there is a great difference between reading the Bible in a living way and reading it in a dead way. You may read a Bible verse in a dead way, reading only the black and white letters, or you can read the same verse in a living and rich way. But this is not to say that we only spend time to read the Bible for the ˀpose of having the supply for the home meetings. Rather, we all need to pay attention to our personal reading of the Bible. If we want the home meetings to be strong, then we ourselves must be strong. If we ourselves are not strong, the home meetings will not be strong either. Because you are those who attend the home meetings, when you come together, you are the home group. If each of you is not strong, does not know how to read the Bible, and does not know how to read the Bible in a living way, how could the home meeting be strong? Therefore, if you are not strong, the home meeting will not be strong. In order for a Christian to be strong, he must live a normal Christian life. Your Bible reading must be living. Every day you must pray, fellowship with the Lord, walk by the Spirit, and live Christ. If you have this kind of living, you will be living not only when you come to the home meeting but even when you are at home.

READING THE BIBLE WITH THE LIFE-STUDY MESSAGES

Many brothers and sisters can testify that eleven years ago we did not have the Life-study Messages. At that time, when we read the Bible and came to a difficult word, we would go from reference book to reference book. That caused our head to swim, and we were still not certain of the real meaning. Thank the Lord, in 1974 in the United States, because of the rapid increase in number among us, the Lord led us to begin the Life-study Messages. In eleven years, we have read through all twenty-seven books of the New Testament. Now the complete set of messages has been printed. Speaking the fact, the contents of these messages are very rich. Not only is every message rich, but even every page is very rich. If you are only willing to use them, to pick one up and read a paragraph, they will be helpful to you. This set of messages is the rich treasure store among us. No matter which book in the New Testament you want to read, I advise you to read it with the Life-study Messages. When you read by yourself, you still do not quite know how to unlock the Bible. But as you put the Life-study Message on that certain chapter or verse alongside the Bible, and read a few lines, you will touch the essence in the Bible. Do not consider that in doing so you are replacing the Bible with the Life-study Messages.

If you read the Bible in this way, you will find that every sentence in the Life-studies supplies the Bible to you. In every line of the Life-studies the Bible as the ingredient has been cooked just as raw rice is cooked for you to eat. This does not mean that as we eat cooked rice, we no longer want the raw rice. But rather, in the Life-studies I have ground soy beans into soy bean milk and have made it into tofu, and I have ground wheat into flour and have steamed it into steamed bread. This set of Life-studies is a key, and it can open the door to the spiritual treasury. It saves a lot of time which you would otherwise spend researching the meaning of words. It is the way to obtain the rich supply and it is also the most time-saving way. If you would try it, you would find that to read the Bible with the Life-studies does not waste any time at all.

SPENDING TWENTY MINUTES EVERY DAY
TO READ THE WORD

You all love the Lord, and you love the church. I believe you all would take my exhortation. I hope that it would not be too much for you to set aside twenty minutes every day to read the Bible with the Life-study Messages. If you are willing to do this, you will discover that it makes a big difference whether or not you read it. Where there is a will, there is a way. Whoever is willing to do it will be able to do it. As long as you have this desire, tell the Lord, "Lord, have mercy on me. Every day, either in the morning or in the evening, give me twenty minutes. I would spend time in Your Word and live before You."

Perhaps some would say that they cannot get up in the morning. But everyone can go to bed late. It is relatively easy to get a lazy one to rise up early. After rolling over a few times, he will get up. But to get an adult to go to bed at 10:30 in the evening is as difficult as restraining a galloping horse. We all know that we should go to bed early. But instead of going to bed we talk a little longer with someone. Then we pick up the newspaper and read for another twenty minutes. Then we may pick up the phone and talk for a few more minutes, and before we know it the time has become late. I often tell others that if they could regain half an hour they spent tarrying here and there, or half an hour of time they wasted, or even shorten their sleeping time half an hour to spend it before the Lord, they would be healthy in body, soul, and spirit.

Today we have come to a crucial point. If we do not build up the home meetings, I can assure you that the church will have no future. The spread of the church is based upon the home meetings, and you are the home meetings. If every one of you can prepare a regular home-cooked meal, the home meetings can surely be built up. The regular home cooking is produced out of your spending half an hour or twenty minutes every day to read the Bible. I suggest that during the twenty minutes you spend reading the Word each day, you read the verses that will be used in the home meetings. Every day prepare at home the material for the home meetings. If the churches all practice this, and every home group practices this, would not the content of the home meetings be rich?

BRINGING THE HOME MEETINGS COMPLETELY OUT OF THE COMMON REALM

As we attend the home meetings, we must bring them out of the common realm: out of the commonness of religion, the commonness of tradition, and the commonness of death. The best way to begin a home meeting is not with Scripture reading, prayer, or singing hymns. The best beginning is to have no beginning. If you arrive at the home meeting before 7:30, you may look at the flowers and the grass outside the window. If you really have a burden to pray, surely you may do so. If a brother comes in and says hello to you, you should stand up quickly and shake hands with him and talk with him. But let us observe one thing together: for the sake of time, when it is 7:30, we should begin the meeting. Our prayer should come out spontaneously, not in a religious way. Twenty minutes after the start of the meeting, let us all pray-read the Bible together. There is no leader in any home meeting, but everyone is a leader. Not only brothers can take the lead, but also sisters. We all should remember to begin pray-reading the Word twenty minutes after the start of the meeting. At this time we should also bring out the Life-studies so that anyone may take the lead to begin reading. Our reading of the Word should not be a dead reading but a living reading. When you have the enjoyment within, just share three or five sentences. When you come to a sentence and receive much supply within, just offer a prayer spontaneously. But you all must remember that whether you pray, give a testimony, or share something, it should not be long. No one should speak longer than two minutes. Meetings like this will surely be rich.

In every home meeting, even though there is no appointed leader, those who prepare something for the meeting are spontaneously the leaders and core members. As every family prepares their meal, there are always one or two who really know how to cook. They should bear the responsibility to do a little more and also bear the responsibility to teach others. Sometimes, it just happens that everyone in a home meeting is a weak one, while in another group there are more strong ones. In this situation one should fellowship with the elders to somewhat balance the strong ones in one area with the weak ones, so that every home meeting has a few core members.

EXPLAINING THE LORD'S WORD IN A SIMPLE WAY TO CREATE A DEEP IMPRESSION IN PEOPLE

Suppose you and I are now going to a home meeting together. I will use the first message from the Life-study of Galatians for a demonstration. When we come to the portion which says, "The books of Galatians, Ephesians, Philippians, and Colossians form a cluster of Epistles, " I would stop and explain a little bit. I would say, "Brothers and sisters, here it says that these four books form a cluster of Epistles. Which are these four books? They are Galatians, Ephesians, Philippians, and Colossians." This is to read and also to explain. Then I would continue to read, ". . . which make up the heart of the divine revelation, in the New Testament." I would then say, "Brothers and

ON HOME MEETINGS

sisters, we have to remember that these four books are the heart." I would then continue the reading: "Therefore, these books are very important. Ephesians covers the church as the Body of Christ, whereas Colossians deals with Christ as the Head of the Body. Galatians is concerned with Christ, and Philippians, with the experience of Christ. In Colossians and Ephesians we receive a clear view of the Head and the Body. In Galatians and Philippians we see Christ and the experience of Christ." As I read in this way, someone who is listening may have an inspiration and say, "This is really good! These few sentences point out clearly the main subjects of Ephesians and Colossians. The book of Ephesians covers the church as the Body of Christ, whereas Colossians deals with Christ as the Head of the Body." While we are speaking like this, we should avoid a preaching tone.

We all know that in Chinese cooking the best dishes are the Peking dishes. Why is this? Because the Peking cooking does not depend on seasonings to enhance the flavor of the food, but it brings out the original flavor of the food. The best way to read the Bible is to not use too much seasoning. Just read the Word in a simple way. In this way people will be more impressed and more touched, and we will save time.

GIVING MORE TIME AND OPPORTUNITY TO THE YOUNG ONES

In addition, one principle we should keep well is that the older ones should not assume their seniority by speaking without ceasing. Let the younger ones speak more. When a family gathers together, everyone would be very happy to hear some words uttered from the mouth of the three- or four-year-old grandaughter, and no one would fall asleep. In the home meetings, time and opportunity must be given to the young ones. One principle which is universally agreed upon is that the progress of human society depends on the second generation. The second generation always stands on the shoulders of the first. In the matter of the truth, the young ones may not know as much as the older ones, but the points that they know are fresher than those the older ones know.

We are advancing rapidly in the learning and studying of the truth. We have coined more than a hundred new terms, such as the essential Spirit, the economical Spirit, the Spirit of power, and many others. Today, every field of learning is advancing, especially among the young people. Therefore, we believe that the future of the church and the freshness and livingness of the meetings all depend on the young ones. We should give the time and opportunity to them. This is an unalterable principle. If the young people are given the opportunity, they will become all the more fresh and spiritually prosperous.

CHAPTER FIVE

THE FUNCTION OF THE HOME MEETINGS

The Bible says that the church is a family. The population of a family can never be very large. In principle a family is different from a kingdom. A kingdom is a unit of many people, but a family is not. On the one hand, the Bible says that the church is God's family; on the other hand, it says that the church is God's kingdom (Eph. 2:19; Matt. 16:18-19). A family is built upon the unit of an individual, while a kingdom is built upon the unit of a family. In order to have a healthy family, there must first be healthy citizens; in order to have a healthy society, there must be healthy families; and in order to produce a strong country, there must be healthy societies. On the one hand, the church is God's kingdom; on the other hand, it is God's family. The base of God's kingdom is built upon the family. Fallen Christianity has neglected the aspect of the family. Since we divided into individual halls, we have not emphasized the family; therefore the increase has been very low. We should follow the Lord's recovery to come back to the beginning, to the unit of the family. When the family unit is strong, the kingdom is strong.

THE CHURCH BEING OF GOD, OF CHRIST, AND OF THE SAINTS

The components of a family are not differentiated into male and female, old and young, or strong and weak. If there is the differentiation of old and young, strong and weak, that is an army. Sometimes we would like our home meetings to be like an army, with all the members being orderly and each one being a fighter. But that is not a family. Some people have an altogether different view of the home meetings. They think, "My home meeting is a gathering together of 'small potatoes.' What can we do? I surely cannot hear a good message." It is wrong to have the concept of supporting home meetings with the desire of being the group leader, and it is also wrong to have the concept of making everyone in the meetings a soldier. Furthermore, we must turn from the concept of going to the home meetings to hear someone else speak. There are many germs and diseases in such concepts.

I would beg the brothers to be calm in their attitude toward the home meetings. We must see that the apostles went out to establish churches, not to establish an apostolic work. After the apostles established the churches, they did not exalt the elders to a high position. In Christianity, as a pastor or preacher goes out to establish churches, the more he does, the more the churches end up on his own shoulders. People in society see a certain group as the church established by paster So-and-so, and they see another group as the church of preacher So-and-so. When he leaves that place, immediately the people who remain become a group of orphans, without a father and without a mother. After not too long, the church also disperses and ceases to exist. Among us there are some elders who, when they administrate the church, the more they administrate, the more the church becomes theirs. The New Testament shows us that the church is the church of God, the church of Christ, and the church of the saints (Acts 20:28; Rom. 16:16; 1 Cor. 14:33). The Bible does not designate the church as the church of the apostles nor the church of the elders.

The apostles said that they preached Christ Jesus as Lord and themselves as slaves of all (2 Cor. 4:5). The apostles are not the lords of the church, but the household slaves in God's house. The workers are not the masters of the church; they are the slaves of all the saints. The saints are God's children. Whenever some become co-workers or apostles, they become the slaves of God's children. This is the truth in the Bible.

In Matthew 20 the Lord Jesus said that among the nations those who are great exercise authority over them, but "it is not so among you" (vv. 25-26). In Matthew 23 the Lord Jesus said that the Pharisees love to take the chief seats, but that we should not be so. The greater among us shall be our servant (vv. 6-11). As the Lord was giving these teachings, Peter must have witnessed with his own eyes and heard with his own ears. Therefore, he wrote these words in 1 Peter 5: "The elders...nor as lording it over the the allotments, but becoming patterns of the flock...and all of you gird yourselves with humility toward one another" (vv. 1, 3, 5). These words are meant to remind us that the elders and apostles are not masters. The masters of the church are, first, God the Father, second, the Lord Jesus, and third, the saints. The ones who administrate the church, lead the church, and even those who raise up the churches, are all slaves. The apostles are slaves, and the elders are slaves. Only the saints are the masters.

In Christianity it is not only the workers, the clergy, and the ones who administrate the church who do not keep their position, but the saints have also forsaken their own position. The saints willingly forsake their position as master. We must always remember that the church is the church of Christ and the church of the saints. The church is absolutely not the church of the co-workers, nor is it the church of the elders. Such a correct understanding of the church matters greatly. When you know that you are the owner of the church, you will certainly do your best to preserve your possession. For example, if a particular house is yours and you are the owner of that house, you will certainly do your best to preserve that house, repairing places where there is damage and fixing spots where there are leaks. However, if that house is rented by you, you would not care for it with all of your heart. Your attitude might be, "If the house leaks, let it leak. If the house is damaged, let it be damaged. As long as I can lie down and sleep, that is good enough. Anyway, it is not my possession. It belongs to someone else."

THE OWNERS OF THE CHURCH BEING THE SAINTS

Dear brothers, all of us must have such a new concept, a new sense that we are the owners of the church. The church being God's kingdom is based upon the church being God's family. It is impossible for the church to be strong without the family being strong. For the family to be strong, every saint needs to be an owner. The co-workers are only household slaves. The one who serves you is not the master. You are the master of the church. On this point, we must not allow fallen Christianity to influence the atmosphere and flavor among us, by making us uplift preachers, elders, and ministers, and to forget that the real masters are the saints. Tonight we are here to do our best to change this concept. If we cannot change this concept, then we are still in the realm of fallen Christianity. We need to see this exceedingly great light. We love the big meetings, but the big meetings are not for the big meetings. The big meetings are for the producing of saints, from which the individual saints are to be built up into a family.

Acts 14 records that the Apostle Paul went out to Iconium, Lystra, and other places, preaching the gospel in every place. Probably in less than a year he went back to establish elders in every place. Those who became elders were all "baby" elders who had been saved for less than a year. The apostle's ultimate concept was to cause the saints to remember clearly that he, the apostle, had no intention of building the church upon himself. He preached the gospel that people might be saved, he established churches in every place, he appointed some to be elders, and then he turned over each local church to the elders of that locality. Parents have a mistaken concept and feeling of always considering their sons and daughters as children. The fathers always feel that their sons cannot do this well and cannot do that well. The mothers always say that their daughters cannot cook. They feel that the daughters do not know how to do it; therefore, they should let the mothers do it. As a result, these sons or daughters actually do not know how to do anything; everyone is like a handicapped person. But under Paul, the "babies" became elders.

THE LORD NOT ESTABLISHING LEADERS
IN THE NEW TESTAMENT

In the New Testament the Lord never appointed a leader to lead. He did appoint twelve apostles, but He did not appoint a chief apostle, nor did He appoint one to call a meeting. In Acts 6 the church appointed seven brothers to serve tables, yet among these seven we cannot find out who was the leader. When the time came for Paul to appoint elders, he did not name a "chief elder." In the practice of the church life, our concept is that among five elders there must be one who is the chief. However, this concept is different from the divine concept, and it is also different from the biblical concept. This concept is to return to the Old Testament. In the Old Testament God's people were under the divine rule. In the Holy of Holies God revealed His heart's desire through the Urim and the Thummim, and then it was passed on to the people through the high priest (Num. 27:21). During those days, there was no king in Israel. Nevertheless, the people wanted to imitate the Gentiles and were willing to have a king to rule over them. Their thought of asking God for a king offended God very much, because that meant that they denied God as their King (1 Sam. 8:4-7). They wanted a visible king, not God. God was their invisible King, the King in their spirit. God wanted them to live in their spirit that they might know God. If they lived in the flesh, they would not be able to know God. Finally, God gave them a king, Saul, who caused them much pain. To set up a king is against the principle of the divine rule. In the church we must not have the thought of having a king. Even the more, we must not have the ambition to be a king.

Some think that among us there must be a strong leader. They think that leader should be set up in order for everyone to have a sense of responsibility. However, that is altogether a human concept. When we practice the home meetings, no one is the head yet everyone has the sense of responsibility. The church is the church of the brothers and of the saints. From now on, every brother and sister must bear the responsibility, because they are the owners of the church. The church belongs to you, to me, and to the saints.

THE NEED FOR BODY-CONSCIOUSNESS IN ADMINSTRATING THE CHURCH

In the past whenever we asked certain brothers to take care of a meeting hall, those who took care of that meeting hall would compete for manpower and financial resources for that hall. Brothers, please remember that when you administrate the church, you are not administrating for that local church, but for Christ's universal Body. If a brother in that local church has the burden to move to South America, you should not restrain him, but rather you should thank the Lord and encourage him, giving him an allowance for travel, family support, and three years' living expenses. If you are willing to do this, the church will be blessed. When we administrate the church, we must have a Body-consciousness and not use our personal judgment to judge anything. According to our concept, Jacob was very bad, but the Lord said, "Jacob I loved, but Esau I hated"(Rom. 9:13; Mal. 1:2-3). According to our way, we want to administrate well the church we are in, but God wants to put South America in good order. On the whole earth there are over six hundred churches. By the Lord's mercy, from the beginning until now I have treated every church alike without discrimination. I hope that you will also have a Body-consciousness. You are here serving the church, not for the service here but for the Lord's Body on the whole earth. I hope that not only the co-workers and elders will have this attitude, this spirit, this feeling, and this flavor, but also that every brother and sister will have the same.

The basic principle of the Lord's building the church is to build up the home meetings as the base. When we go to a home meeting we should never have an attitude that when we go to raise up that home meeting, we go to take the lead. You should go to a home meeting to strengthen it, to enrich it, but you should not go there to be the head.

Because you go there to function, and you supply the meeting more than others, naturally in the Lord's eyes you are a pillar in that home meeting, and that home meeting has become strong because you have functioned. But on your side, you just went to function without any thought of being the leader.

ALL THE MEMBERS
DEVELOPING THEIR SPIRITUAL GIFTS

The Bible clearly shows us that the Lord did not expressly set up any person to be the head, in order that all the members would develop their own spiritual gifts. In the process of natural development, the stronger ones would bear more responsibility. It is the same in principle with respect to the home meetings, the individual meeting halls, and the church. Then the Lord can have a way here, and we can come out of organization. This light among us should be very bright. In the church, first, we have no organization; second, we have no hierarchy. We do not have the higher-ups controlling the people below, nor do we have the people below following the higher-ups. Our relationship is not that of superiors to inferiors. We have no organization, but we have contact and fellowship.

Because of our way of arranging the leadership in the past, through these few decades and through a long period of suffering we have discovered that there are many shortcomings. Not only have the brothers and sisters not been perfected, but even the leading ones have not been perfected. When I reconsider the entire New Testament concerning these things, I see that the Lord has never set up leaders. Therefore, by the Lord's grace we should let the saints develop much in gifts. As a result of the development, some will naturally be manifested to be stronger, and some weaker. Then the stronger ones will bear more responsibility, while the weaker ones will also take care of their portion of the responsibilities. Consequently, the ones bearing more responsibility will naturally become the pillars. Now we hope that all the brothers will embrace this attitude and have this kind of spirit, to positively get into

the home meetings and to function according to the gift
that the Lord has measured to you. If the measure the Lord
has given to you is more, then spontaneously you are the
pillar in that home meeting. As long as you put forth
faithfully what the Lord has given you, your function will
be fulfilled. Then the Lord will gain ground in you, and the
church will also receive benefit because of you.

THE BASIC SUPPLY IN THE MEETINGS
COMING FROM THE WORD OF GOD
AND THE SPIRIT OF GOD

The basic supply in a meeting comes from God's Word;
the basic vitality, motivation, or power in a meeting comes
from the Holy Spirit. The Lord has given us two great
gifts: one is His divine Word, which is the Bible; the other
is the Holy Spirit, who is the source of our motivation,
vitality, and power. Whether it be a big meeting or a small
meeting, for the meeting to be rich and strong there must
be the word of the Lord and the Spirit. Some think that if
you have the Holy Spirit, you have the Lord's word.
Actually, to pay attention to the Spirit without the Lord's
Word results in poverty. The Bible says that the word is
related to the Spirit (Eph. 6:17; John 6:63). For all these
years, the reason we in the Lord's recovery have been so
blessed by the Lord has been because of the Lord's word
and the Lord's truth.

In the home meetings we must promote the Lord's Word.
To make our meetings strong and rich, we must learn to
use the Life-studies. The Life-studies can assist us in our
Bible study in the same way that a good machine can
assist us in accomplishing something. The Life-study is in
your hand; you need to learn how to use it. We hope that in
two meetings a home meeting would finish one Life-study
Message. When you attend the home meeting, you must
not divide the message rigidly: you see that it has eight
pages, so you read four this time and four the next time,
like a quack doctor performing a surgery. Instead, you
should consider the sections. The first time you read a new
book, you have to study the background. The second time

you should study the subject. If we intend to study the Life-studies well in the home meetings, when we come to points of truth in messages, we need to speak them properly, emphasizing the important points and spending a little more time on them. In this way the message can be studied thoroughly.

It is even better if, before the home meeting, every brother and sister would read the message once, and have some digestion and prior preparation. During the meeting, the brothers who are the core members, who are stronger in knowledge, richer in life, and better in utterance, should all bear the responsibility to explain the new terms so that everyone can receieve the benefit. When it comes to the crucial points, there may be some spontaneous pray-reading. At this time if some are touched, some prayers can be offered. Or perhaps some, after hearing the words of the message, may recall their past experiences and offer some fellowship. Or some, having eaten and having been satisfied, may recall a song with grace in their hearts, and everyone may sing together. If there is no song and no inspiration, do not just carelessly select a hymn to sing. This is like forcing a denture into someone's mouth.

THE HOME MEETINGS BEING THE TOUCHSTONE OF THE BUILDING OF THE CHURCH

We see clearly that the building of the church is based on home meetings. Then who builds the home meetings? Not the co-workers nor the elders, but the brothers and sisters. The home meeting is the touchstone (a test for determining the quality or genuineness) of the building of the church. The church is built on this foundation.

According to the present situation, the first thing that the home meetings need to do is to restore those who have not been meeting for a long time. We hope that all the brothers and sisters will be mobilized to seek out, according to their addresses, those who have not been meeting for a long time and restore them to attend the home meetings. The second thing is to motivate every brother and sister, whether old or young, as long as he has a house, to open his house at least once every two weeks. You should have a gospel meeting in the home every other week. You need to gradually educate and enlighten people in the home meetings, providing them with the gospel materials and encouraging them to speak for the Lord and to open their homes. From house to house, every house should preach the gospel. The third thing is to do your best to keep people coming to the meetings. When a person comes, stick to that one; you must keep him. The responsibility for keeping people cannot rest on the elders, co-workers, or a few people. The responsibility for keeping the people must rest on the home meeting, that is, on all the brothers and sisters. This is a great responsibility for the home meeting. The fourth thing is to strengthen the home meetings. To have rich meetings, you must work the Lord's word richly into the home meetings. The fifth thing is to cause the home meetings to reach God's purpose for the church. The Lord desires to gain a living Body to express Him on the earth.